Elements of Innovation

A collection of articles on how to achieve innovation in mid-sized and smaller companies

Published by Center for Simplified Strategic Planning, Southport, Connecticut

www.cssp.com

Simplified Strategic Planning is a registered trademark of the Center for Simplified Strategic Planning, Inc.

Printed in the United States of America

Duncan, J. Peter
Elements of Innovation
Work / Peter Duncan (editor), with Tom Ambler, Dana Baldwin, Robert Bradford, and Denise Harrison

1. Management. 2. Strategic Planning.

ISBN 0-9725605-5-6

The **Center for Simplified Strategic Planning, Inc.** is a consulting firm which specializes in making outstanding strategic planning a do-able reality for many companies. CSSP, Inc. offers a seminar, *Simplified Strategic Planning for Small to Mid-Sized Companies,* to teach interested companies the Simplified Strategic Planning process. The seminar, which is presented over forty times a year across the country, is the most popular seminar of its kind in the United States. In addition, CSSP professionals participate directly with the managers of about one hundred companies to assist in developing and implementing their specific strategic plans to achieve superior results.

Contents

Editor's Introduction

The concept of innovation is a key element of success in any business. For it is through innovation that value is created and an enterprise renews itself. Without innovation, a business will die.

While creativity is essential to innovation, it is not the whole story. Many creative ideas have failed to produce innovation because the company did not have in place a process to capture and develop these ideas into something that brought the idea to fruition in the market. Thus, you will find these articles address both how to generate the creative spark that is the seed of innovation, as well as the process of innovation that is the tree that grows from the seed.

Too often innovation is thought of only in terms of "new products", but, in fact, it should permeate all aspects of a business. There is often tremendous value that can be unlocked with innovations in sales, administration, operations, distribution, customer service, and marketing.

These articles identify the essential environmental elements that must be considered and put in place to foster innovation in a mid-sized or smaller company. They explore concepts for stimulating creative ideas and the process for bringing those ideas into commercial practice as well as measuring the results from innovation efforts.

We hope you enjoy the articles and we welcome your comments or questions at the e-mail addresses listed below.

Peter Duncan, editor
November 2003

Put yourself out of business

by J. Peter Duncan

It is a company-eat-company world.

Everyday your rivals try to offer something better that will attract more customers to their services or products. Everyday you try to hold them off. You *hope* your offerings are better, but that can only last so long. Eventually competitors can find a way to surpass your current offerings unless you innovate and further raise the challenges they must overcome.

It's a Darwinian game where the victors are allowed to continue on to innovate again and move their industries forward. For the losers, irrelevance, obsolescence and ultimately business failure is all too common a fate. If you were to examine the Fortune 500 list from 1955 (the first year it was published) there would be some companies that you would recognize, but many more (well over 25% of the list) that went the way of the dinosaurs and became extinct-dying of changes in their environment or being gobbled up by more aggressive carnivores. This is frequently the fate of the largest organizations in the business world, and the challenge for survival is even greater for the small and mid-sized companies.

To survive, a company must be aware of its environment and alert to change. Change - it is everywhere. It is the current of business, sweeping over all like a flooding river. When it rages, it is frightening: bumping, bruising and even drowning those with its power. When it is calm, change is tolerable, and we build structures - systems, models and policies - that try to control and resist it. If we get a good thing going, instinct tells us to lock in the gains - to keep doing more of the same to capitalize on our success. But it is a fine line between capitalizing on success, and getting stuck in a rut while clinging to a dream of a past when business was easier.

But there are companies that get tired of clinging and embrace change. They prefer the adventure of moving with the current of business over clinging and dying of boredom. Letting go, they embark on a voyage into an unknown future where they are often tumbled and smashed into unknown obstacles. For some it is too much and they stop and cling again. But for those who refuse to hold on, they soar with the currents appearing to magically fly above those who try to resist the current of change.

Which kind of company will you create? One that uses its energy and resources to hold back the currents of change, or one that risks the currents of change to create new value in business? This is the challenge of innovation. The best strategies always hinge on some form of innovation.

What is so great about Innovation?

A dictionary defines "innovation" as the introduction of something new or different. According to the eminent strategy professor, James Bryan Quinn, "Innovation is the first reduction to practice of an idea in a culture." Without innovation, all we can do is try to optimize what we have, but in a world where competitors are constantly upping the ante, this is not sufficient. Innovation is the thing that gets you ahead of the pack, rather than chasing your rivals. It is the source of mutation in the DNA of a company that is essential to survival in a changing environment.

Innovation can take on many forms. Most often people think of product innovation - the new idea that gives your offering an advantage over a rival's. This is a good start, but it is a rather narrow use of a powerful concept. What are new processes you can use to transform the very way in which value is created in your industry? Amazon.com latched on to the Internet as a whole new concept of a retail selling. Are there services you could offer which would be innovations in your industry? General Electric strives to wrap services around every physical product it sells. And at the highest level, can you invent and deploy a strategy that changes the rules of the game for your business? Wal-Mart has redefined customer service and relentlessly driven down costs to build a company with "everyday low prices" that has rocketed to the top of the Fortune 500 while rivals Sears and K-mart struggle to shore up their strategies which brought them success in the 1970's.

Innovation is at the heart of value creation. In each case, someone or some group of people imagined a company different from the status quo. A new idea was translated into a product, service, concept or strategy that could be brought into practice to create new value for the company. Not all innovations are successful. While any particular innovation may succeed or fail, any company that wants to be successful must be working on some kind of innovation to build a sustainable advantage.

If Innovation is so great why doesn't everyone do it? Well, there are a small number of companies that either don't understand the need to innovate or don't care to try. But among those trying to get ahead, there seem to be two common reasons companies fail to innovate.

The first reason is that they are successful. Mankind's instinct is not to rock the boat when you have a good thing going. When a company does innovate, they are proud of their success. They want to capture full advantage of the good times and try to control the environment to extend their winning streak. Rather than investing in the next innovation, they get trapped into preserving the advantage of their last innovation.

In the 1970's IBM developed the most successful business

model for building and selling large powerful computers to corporations. Success made the "mainframe" division of IBM very powerful, and they used this power to try to preserve their dominance in the market. Rather than forging ahead with daring new products built from the latest technology, the IBM mainframe group became conservative, slowly adding emerging technology onto their existing platform. Digital Equipment Corporation had no existing platform. They were able to start from scratch and design the best possible computer. From this innovative quest the "mini computer" emerged and DEC rode to prominence on this product during the 1980's. But like IBM, DEC allowed its success to slip into arrogance as they reveled in the innovation, which brought them success and turned a blind eye to the ongoing march of technology into the PC market. Tasks that once needed a mini-computer migrated to the PC and HP, Compaq, Dell and others took share from DEC. In time, DEC was so weak that they were unable to bring their innovations to market and Compaq acquired them.

The second reason companies don't innovate is, like DEC in the later years, they get caught in a competitive squeeze. It often begins with a sudden competitive attack on a market. A rival innovates and introduces a product of greater value, but prices it equal to the incumbent, or they bring a product of similar value, but offer it at a much lower price point. In either case the quickest and most common response is a price cut on existing product to preserve market share and cash flow.

Any arbitrary price cut has to be followed with cost reduction, to get profitability back to acceptable levels. All to often, this means downsizing and reining in investment, both of which take resources away from innovation efforts. Companies get fixated on improving ROI by managing the denominator (investment) rather than pushing innovation driven numerator of the equation. This leaves a company less able to innovate and more susceptible to the next competitive squeeze. Before long they can find themselves on a downward spiral like the American automakers or Pan Am Airlines in the 1980's. AT&T failed to prevail against rivals in the early 1990's and found itself squeezed and had to resort to breaking up the company to improve its ROI when it was unable to deliver a breakthrough innovation toward the end of the decade.

What does it take to be innovative?

An innovator is never satisfied. There is always something better around the corner, and he is determined to break from the pack and find it. An innovator seeks not only to beat the competition, but also to better his own inventions. In company terms, an innovative company needs to try to put itself out of business (with new ideas) before someone else does it to them.

Suppose you were in the port-a-potty business. It is not a business that most people want to stick their nose in. I don't recall ever meeting someone who was really satisfied with their experience using a port-a-potty, so it would seem there is plenty of demand for a breakthrough innovation. So far the industry leaders seem to have made improvements that help them lower their costs- easy to clean plastic, rugged commercial design. But other than more powerful deodorizers, there has not been much innovation to improve the consumer's experience.

So how would you innovate to try to put the industry leaders out of business??

Well Potty Palooza asked and answered the question with a determination to change the basis of competition in the industry. Their approach, install 27 private bathrooms with modern porcelain flush toilets, running water, air conditioning and luxury hardwood floors in an 18-wheeler trailer. Not only do they provide the basic facilities, but also each of their trailers has a full time attendant to periodically clean and stock the rest rooms. Will it work? I don't know, but it is the type of redefinition of an industry that has the possibility of being a transformational breakthrough. Rather than following the leaders with incremental improvements, they have attempted to fundamentally change the rules of the game and set a new basis for competition in their industry. They are engaged in the imagination game, not the imitation game. What about you? How will you change the rules of your industry?

Increase your innovation quotient (IQ)

Okay, so you get the idea… when we speak of innovation we are talking about introducing significant new ideas that redefine the basis of competition. But how does a mid-size or smaller company do that? You can't afford a think tank like Bell Labs.

The good news is that innovation is not dependent on dollars. Sure some money will help bring things to market, but the fundamental building blocks of innovation are IDEAS, KNOWLEDGE and A PROCESS for translating these into tangible services and products in the market. Every person in your company has the ability to contribute regardless of function, title or salary, IF you establish a culture and an environment to encourage innovation.

Once you have a suitable environment, you need to fill it with creative and qualified people. The most innovative companies like 3M and Microsoft often interview 100 qualified candidates to find the one that will fit with the culture and become a contributor to their value creation process. In addition to the people and the environment, you need to organize for the type of innovation you are trying to encourage. Incremental innovation has a 1-2 year time horizon and is often driven by strong egos, bonus compensation and a small quick acting team. Where as breakthrough innovations have a 7-20 year time horizon and are best facilitated by a creating a stable large team that is a collegial peer group that respect each other and will stay together over the duration of the program. In all cases innovation comes from the coupling of a breakthrough idea with a disciplined process to refine and improve the idea to make it commercially viable.

To inspire innovation in your business, there are three types of knowledge you want to encourage and capture:

- Know What....cognitive knowledge
- Know How.....advanced skills
- Know Why.....systems understanding

These are the raw materials of innovation. By the way, they are also the building blocks of your strategic competencies. The best companies develop and institutionalize knowledge in the company. So if you have been developing strategic competencies, you should be well on your way to having the elements of an innovation.

But these are just the raw materials. The real genius of innovation comes when someone dips into this collection of ideas with a net and draws a select group together for a particular purpose. At Canon they drew together their knowledge of optics, electromechanical systems and mass production to launch the innovative personal photocopier when Xerox and its competitors were still thinking the market was about big, high speed, fully featured machines.

The inspiration for innovation happens in an instant. It is impossible to predict the exact moment or elements required for genius to strike. There are, however, some common places to look for inspiration. You should examine:

- needs/demands of market place (customers provide some of the best ideas)
- value chain analysis (define linkages and where value is created)
- figures of merit (define what it takes to win)
- theoretical limits, bounds
- trends (extrapolation of pacing parameters)
- models (interaction of a number of factors)
- attack ourselves (define how we could beat our best today)

But inspiration is just the start. Good companies have a

disciplined process to transform the genius of a moment into a refined product or service that is ready for the market. This often requires several rounds of development with creative inputs at each stage. The culture of the company has to not only support the free thinking geniuses that seed the innovation process with ideas, but also the more linear development folks who reduce the idea into practice. The best companies find ways to link their innovation process with their strategy process so the two define and support a single vision for the organization. They also find ways to measure innovation so they can objectively monitor their progress and strive for ever higher performance.

Keep yourself in business

The best way to keep yourself in business is to try to put yourself out of business. If you are always on edge, never complacent, then you will challenge your team for continuous improvement. Innovation requires vision, inspiration and the patience to support a relatively long time horizon. You can encourage it by creating a productive environment and organizational structure that you fill with the best people.

Change is a constant in business. We need to continually change and evolve if we are to survive. Static barriers don't keep out the barbarians who want our business. Winners embrace change and create moving barriers that keep their rivals off balance. True barriers to entry are created not by one thing, but by the RATE at which you innovate and keep your competitors struggling to catch up.

Winners learn to plan the imagination game that leads to innovation. They learn to have their cake, and *eat it before someone else does*. Winners assume that others are trying to take their customers at every turn and that their very survival is at stake. They figure out time and time again how to put themselves out of business before their rivals do. That is the challenge of not just a strategy, but a renewable and sustainable strategic basis for a successful business.

Creating an Environment for Innovation

by M. Dana Baldwin

Once your company has made a conscious decision to encourage innovation, where and how should you start? How do you encourage people in every part of the company to innovate? In this article, one assumes that one has agreed on a consistent definition of what it means to innovate, and that one has the intention of involving as many in the company as possible and appropriate.

ATMOSPHERE:

Innovation needs a good atmosphere in which to develop. It is definitely a cultural characteristic and must be encouraged and nurtured inside a company. It does not come by simply flipping a switch. One must set an environment that encourages people to think in unusual and creative ways. This is not easy to accomplish when much of business is, by definition, so structured and orderly in its processes. Business, whether products- or services-oriented, needs to have somewhat standardized routines for much of what it needs to accomplish. Innovation, on the other hand, requires thinking out of the ordinary. These two are so different that in order to have effective innovation, care must be taken to encourage and allow unconventional thinking.

Who is responsible for setting the atmosphere for effective innovation? The CEO and top management team must create the environment. They are responsible for establishing a vision (strategy) which embraces innovation. For too many companies, vision or strategy is underrated. Without a vision of where the company is going, often there can be limited success in innovation. Management must create the challenge, the inspiration to push people to stretch, to make the current box bigger. At the same time it must be realistic. For example, a caterpillar can become a butterfly, but not an eagle. The CEO must see his/her job as creating employee excitement and passion, not just as measuring employee satisfaction or financial performance. If one defines the company as more of the same, that's all one gets.

In the book: <u>Orbiting the Giant Hairball</u>, by Gordon MacKenzie, the author tells of an artist who traveled to many different grade schools, showing the students how to do many different kinds of art. His experience is telling: In First Grade, when he asked the question, "Are there any artists here?" he got an overwhelming response. Virtually all the kids enthusiastically put up their hands, eagerly wanting to be recognized as artists. By Second Grade, the response was uniformly around 50% of the class putting their hands up, and by Third Grade the response was only about 10 out of 30 kids who put up their hands. In his analysis of what was happening, the author reasoned that the balance of the kids, those who did not put up their hands, had become "normalized". What he meant is they had learned to think in an acceptable, "normal" way, and no longer considered themselves to be out of the ordinary. In their view, someone who was considered to be an artist was not someone who was normal. Over the last century or so we have allowed ourselves to accept being "normal" and have lost some of the spark of creativity and spontaneity that we start out with as kids. To help bring your company back into the realm of allowing spontaneity and encouraging creativity will be a big challenge. There are many exercises that can help with this transition. If your company suffers from too much "normalcy", you can do some research to bring in the kinds of thought exercises and processes which will help your people shed some of their inhibitions and become more creative.

COMMUNICATION:

One key component of this process is knowledge within the company. The better everyone in the company understands the goals and objectives of the company, the better this process of innovation should be. Internal communication, based on openness and with trust developed over years, is a key to setting this atmosphere. This may well not be a strength in many companies. In a recent article in the Grand Rapids Press newspaper, a well-known local company was profiled. In the article, one of the key workers in the shop would not share his personal knowledge about his job for two reasons. First, he was afraid that management would use the knowledge to redesign his job and force him to work flat-out all day. Second, he was afraid that management would take the knowledge and outsource the work, putting him out of a job. Stepping back to look at this situation, one might well suspect that there is little or no trust of management by the workforce. Can you imagine trying to develop an atmosphere in which innovation and creativity are encouraged without succeeding at changing this low level of trust into something much more positive? A change like this will take many years and much hard work on the part of the entire company, not just management, in order to get to the level of trust required to get people to open up and really participate effectively.

CHALLENGE:

Top management must encourage innovation by setting forth one or more challenges to the appropriate people. Without a challenge, there may be no drive to innovate, nothing to provide the impetus. One familiar example is the challenge that President John F. Kennedy gave the nation when he told Congress that it was his intention that the United States would put a man on the moon by the end of the decade (of the 60s), and bring him back to Earth safely. That one challenge opened a wide ranging set of doors for this country. Think of all the inventions, developments and advances we have gotten from that one challenge. Transistors, micro-electronics, medical monitoring devices, telecommunications devices and many more inventions and developments all came out of the space race. Without the overriding goal set forth and effectively communicated by President Kennedy, it is unlikely that all of these inventions would have come along as quickly as they did. The resulting higher levels of technology have changed the way we live, the way we do business and especially the way we communicate. Many of them might well have been developed in due course, but over what time periods and at what cost to society? With the specific challenge issued by President Kennedy, the needs and preferences of the contributors to the project became known and addressed. And this is what needs to happen in your company if innovation is to happen.

SOURCES OF IDEAS:

In earlier articles in this publication, we have discussed brainstorming as a source for the ideas for the innovation process. But where do the ideas that are brought out in the brainstorming session come from? One area is inside the company. Your fellow employees are most often a good resource for ideas for improvements in internal processes, product improvements, service improvements and customer contact improvements. They are often the ones in the trenches who see the possible problems in the products, processes or services. Internal communications are critical to the effectiveness of this process.

Another idea source is the customer. Knowledge of customers' preferences is absolutely critical. Very few companies can innovate effectively without comprehensive knowledge of their customers' needs and preferences. By some estimates, roughly 50% of all innovations come from customers. What are you doing to get close enough to your customers that you can tap them for ideas? This effort needs to be an on-going, real effort, not a quickie, one time shotgun blast to see what can be dragged in. You need to be cultivating enough of a relationship with your customers that you have two-way communication flowing on a regular basis. You need to have programs in place that will allow and encourage your customers to communicate with you, not just when they have a problem, but when they have a success as well. You should encourage your customers to use you as a resource, even when you do not have the product or service they need. When you get to the point where they call you and ask for guidance on something they know you don't offer, you have earned their respect and you have established reliable and effective communications. Take advantage of this relationship to help you both. Ask for feedback and constructive criticism. Ask for their ideas about what they and others will need in the future. Put these ideas through the same filters you put your own ideas through. Many will not be earthshaking in their potential, but one or two might be the catalyst for the true winner down the road. Effective listening can make a tremendous difference, so you need to train your customer interface people to hear what your customers are saying, not just the words.

PROCESSES:

In addition to an encouraging atmosphere, there must be some procedures established to channel the innovation process. This sounds like a contradiction in definitions, but unstructured thoughts, while necessary for brainstorming, can lead to missed opportunities and wasted resources in much of the innovative process. In general, the creative process is reasonably well structured. It starts with setting the environment to encourage idea generation. This requires focus in particular areas of interest, so that there is not a dilution of concentration. Brainstorming for ideas is next, with the one rule that there are no bad ideas. The reason for this is really quite simple. If we introduce any judgment of ideas at this part of the process, we will surely discourage the creative thinking needed for truly creative thought. As a result, we will likely limit the effectiveness of the brainstorming and, more importantly, the synergy of idea development. At times, someone's off-the-wall idea which, by itself, will have no chance of being adopted, will stimulate a truly creative, effective idea in someone else's mind that might turn out to be the real winner for the company. Please recognize that the innovation process is typically demand driven, that is, it is usually responding to the needs and preferences of the customer. While structured to a point, it is nevertheless chaotic at times, often delivering the unexpected. Whereas, in the normal course of business, the logical, organized types often excel and prevail, in the type of thinking needed for true innovation, the leaders are often those who are firebrands and free thinkers, those with the unusual mind. Their ideas often create suspicion and opposition (i.e.... We've never done it that way before!). To be successful often means that the process requires crusaders and those who will champion a project with passion and drive.

Please note that these ideas do not need to be focused on the products or services the company presents to the market place; they can be directed to the internal processes of the company as well. Productivity improvements, internal process improvements, quality improvements are all fair game for this process. Any appropriate way to lower costs, increase quality and respond better and more quickly help obtain and retain customers, and after all, it is the customers who pay the bills.

TIME HORIZONS:

Depending on the amount of time required for something to be thought up, developed, tested and brought to market, your approach may be quite different. With short horizon projects, the number of people and the scope of the project will of necessity be small. (See table on page 30). As time horizons expand, so does the size of the team, the type of innovation and the scope of the project. The incentives also grow in proportion to the scope of the project, and the risk most likely does, too.

CONCLUSION:

Setting an atmosphere in which innovation is encouraged is often highly correlated with the long term success of a company. Each of the elements explained above is critical to the effective innovation process. Challenge yourself and your senior management team to develop the skills and the atmosphere in which effective innovation becomes a part of your ongoing strategic planning. It is highly probable that your long term survival and viability depend on it.

Time Horizon	1-2 Years	3-6 Years	7-20 Years
Type of Innovation	incremental	step function - longer term platform for annual features and options	breakthrough
Incentive	individual basis this year's profits	team basis medium term options with matched vesting period	personal security, salary tenure, fame, secure retirement, sabbaticals, long vesting stock
Team Size	small (1-3)	bigger (10-100)	very large
Mgt. Style	fast, decisive, ego driven	team-based consensus	bureaucratic, nuturing
Price/Marketing	skim pricing with mark downs	price for volume to get down experience curve first, target price	price for long term profits, defensive - keep others out, monopoly prices if protected

Adapted from lecture by J. B. Quinn, 1994

Innovation - where to look for it
by Denise A. Harrison

Many companies struggle when trying to develop new and creative ideas. Why? It is difficult to think "outside the box," especially in challenging times when it seems you are running as hard and fast as possible just to keep up. But finding successful innovation often is the key to getting off the treadmill. Here are some places to look:

1. Assess your customers' unmet needs and preferences— is there anything new?
2. Assess your strategic competencies—can you use the knowledge base that you have developed in one industry to please a different market segment or industry?
3. Look at emerging trends— does a trend make sense, melded with your company's traditional strengths?
4. Look at technology other industries are adopting—is there a smart way to capitalize on developments that you can tailor for your applications?

Assess Your Customers' Unmet Needs

Water Pik Technologies, Inc.
Personal Health Care Division

Many of Dr. Gerald Moyer's patients developed problems with their gums as they aged. Dr. Moyers, a dentist in Ft. Collins, CO, speculated that these problems could be alleviated if there was a way to clean the gum area of food particles and bacteria. And, the cleaning technology could use a jet of water not only to rid the area of food particles, but also to massage the gums. The massaging action leads to enhanced circulation and healthier gums. Dr. Moyer knew that a jet of water could provide all of the desired benefits—but where could he find a motor that would drive such an invention? He went to a number of sources looking for the proper motor to drive the water to irrigate and massage the gum area. He finally discovered John W. Mattingly, a hydraulic engineer and Colorado State University professor, who was interested in the project. They tried many different options and finally decided upon a piston, hollowed and flared. Their work was a success, but the motor did not produce a constant jet stream of water. Instead it delivered a pulsating stream.

In spite of the fact that the two set out to develop a product with a constant stream of water, the two inventors found the pulsating stream produced the desired effect. Even better— the accidental pulsating made the product potentially patentable. They decided to move forward with the pulsating water stream and developed Water Pik's foundation product: the oral irrigator.

Now the invention was ready for testing, Dr. Moyer distributed oral irrigators to several of his dental patients.

Patients found the product effective, and one patient in particular, Gene Rouse, believed that the oral irrigator was a commercially viable product. So, Gene Rouse set out to find investors to fund the marketing and production necessary to launch this product. Who were the original investors? Dentists, of course! Once he raised the needed funds, Gene Rouse became the first president of Water Pik (at that time called Aqua Tec).

Now the founders were ready to launch the product to its target audience, the dental community. The team decided the fastest way to gain exposure would be to display the oral irrigator at the annual dental convention. The product generated a high level of interest and sales at the show. The company expanded its distribution channel to dental supply dealers. As the oral irrigator became a mainstream product, the company developed retail channels including drug, appliance, and hardware distributors. Soon the product was on retail shelves and consumers could purchase oral irrigators without a visit to the dentist.

The original investors saw the product's success and wanted to cash in their investment. They sold the company to Los Angeles based Teledyne, Inc. in 1976, the same year that Water Pik received the patent on the pulsating oral irrigator product.

With patent in hand, the Water Pik team developed new uses for the irrigator technology including a surgical jet lavage used in Vietnam to cleanse wounds.

Capitalize on Strategic Competencies:

The Original Shower Massage ™
The next real breakthrough came with the development of **The Original Shower Massage™.**

Integrate the pulsating motion of multiple oral irrigators into a showerhead and what do you have? The Original Shower Massage ™! Use an existing Water Pik strategic competency (pulsating water) in a new application—will it work? Will the market accept this novel idea?
As is the case with new concepts, the developer had difficulty convincing the skeptics that **The Original Shower Massage™** would sell. As part of the large conglomerate Teledyne, Water Pik needed corporate approval to invest funds in further developing production capabilities and in a promotional plan to bring this innovative product to market.

When Water Pik presented the new product concept to Corporate, it met a resounding "No!" The Teledyne corporate staff did not believe in the product concept. Showerheads were only installed when a house was built or during a bathroom renovation – consumers would not buy showerheads as a specialty item.

The Water Pik team thought that corporate might throw cold water on this innovative idea, so they went to plan B: the team offered to buy the concept from Teledyne for the amount already invested in development—approximately $175,000. Corporate was faced with a dilemma. Should they let the team buy the concept or fund the production and promotion? Seeing that the team believed firmly in the concept, Teledyne decided to fund the shower massage product.

Smooth sailing from here?

No such luck. The first batch of completed products did not make it to market. Gene Rouse stopped the product before it was shipped. Why? Surprisingly, the shower massage did not have a regular speed mode. Mr. Rouse felt strongly that the product needed a normal, along with fast and slow massage modes, to be attractive to consumers. The team quickly tooled up to make the product enhancements and this improved version of the product went to market. Did consumers embrace the new concept of a shower massage? Yes, the product was the first significant innovative product launch in the shower fixture category in years. The rest is history.

In addition to using its competency in pulsating water jets, Water Pik used its existing sales channels to distribute the product to consumers. Backed by an advertising campaign and point of sale demonstrations (consumers could actually put their hands in a glove and feel the pulsating shower massage), the product introduction was a rousing success.

Today's Market

After many years the shower fixture market is still expanding. Water Pik Technologies (now spun off from Allegheny, who purchased Teledyne in 1999) continues to introduce innovative enhancements to the shower market. Recent introductions include:

1. The Original Shower Massage™ now has 4-8 settings.
2. The New Visions™ product line adds design and styling to the Waterpik™ line.
3. The Cascadia™ and AquaFall™ products provide a drenching experience.
4. Shower panels attach multiple sprayers to the wall, providing four or more heads.
5. Misting Massage offers a spa experience.
6. Medallion™ is a shower room and trade series of products.
7. Slide bars, shower accessories, broaden the line.

Keys to success: developing a competency that met an emerging need (the first oral irrigator) and then using that competency to develop a new product for a category not previously served by Water Pik, shower fixtures.

Manufacturing and Selling Plumbing Pipes—Look at Distribution, Evaluate the Buying Experience

Eric De Jeung sat with the HVAC fittings distributor and reflected on the proposal in front of him. If he could increase sales he would be rewarded handsomely for his efforts. If not, he would earn nothing. This was a commodity product in a crowded market. It would be difficult to increase sales, but times were tough and there was a significant upside to the proposal. Eric accepted the offer.

How can you differentiate your company in a commodity market?
Eric decided to visit various building and plumbing supply houses that sold the company's products to see if there were any unmet needs or ways that the company could differentiate itself.

He observed the contractors buying their supplies; he asked if there were any changes that could be made to improve the product. The contractors were satisfied with the basic product functionality, but they were very frustrated by the buying process. He saw that many contractors had to return to the supply house to exchange products from incorrectly filled orders. This caused down time on the job site. He also noticed that the building supply houses did not know how much inventory they had on hand, often causing builders to walk away empty-handed when items were out of stock.

Eric realized the supply houses were employing the cheapest labor possible to fill orders. The people in order fulfillment were not trained in construction and often had poor math and reading skills. It was this low skill level that caused both problems:

1. Fulfilling orders with incorrect products
2. Inadequate inventory

Eric knew that if he could solve these problems his firm's products would become the supplies of choice.
How do you solve problems at the distribution level?

Order Fulfillment—Fill Orders Correctly—An Emerging Trend

Eric knew that, despite his encouragement, the building supply houses would not hire a more expensive, better-educated, workforce. He needed to develop an innovative approach. He needed to think outside the box—or at least think about the box. What did he do? He changed his product packaging. He placed a picture of every product on every package. Then Eric supplied the counter help with matching charts, and as contractors placed orders they would simply point to the products on the chart and the fulfillment clerk would fill the order by matching the picture on the chart to the picture on the box! The pictures and charts provided a win-win for everyone.

Inventory Control—Counting Made Easy

Now for the inventory problem—products came boxed in packages of 12. Eric knew that service counter clerks could count the number of packages in inventory, but lacked the skills to multiply the numbers by twelve. Why not packages of 10? With boxes of 10, even the simplest clerk could count the boxes, add a zero, and have a correct inventory count. Problem solved—the building supply house owners knew when they needed to order more of Eric's products. They could easily calculate the number of Eric's products on the shelf and make sure that they ordered more when stocks ran low.

By changing the packaging, using product pictures, and having 10 fixtures in each box, Eric resolved both problems and now:

1. Building supply houses were able to keep track of inventory.
2. Builders received the correct fixtures.

Within one year Eric's company became the market leader with 60% share of the market - not too shabby in a commodity business. The key to innovation is not always found in a new product, or a new product feature. It is often found in the buying or the distribution process. How can you make the sale easier for your customer, your distributor? If you can answer this question you may have the key to your future success.

Technology—how can it work for you?
The sharp sword of "bleeding edge" technology has cut many companies. But does this mean you should stay away from technology as a possible source of innovation? Why not adopt a technology currently in use in another industry? With the bugs already out of the new technology, you can focus on its application to your process, products and markets. Here are several examples of companies who have developed applications using technologies already debugged by someone else.

RFID Technology

RFID, radio frequency identification, recognizes consumers

by their unique identification tag and is able to automatically debit a specific consumer's account for a specific transaction.

An early application of RFID technology enhanced the NY/NJ toll collection system. E-ZPass automatically identifies cars passing through tollbooths and debits each car owner's account for the toll. Capitalizing on the NY/NJ RFID application, Mobil (now Exxon/Mobil) is using this technology in its Speedpass™ program. This program allows Speedpass™ customers to simply wave their "Speedpass™" at an electronic reader to have it debit the customer's account for gas or any convenience item. The transaction convenience increased sales significantly. "An average Speedpass™ transaction is more than double the cash amount." NYT, 7/7/02
What's next? Speedpass™ at McDonald's! Fast food faster!

Spreading the use of RFID technology to new applications shows how technology developed for use in one industry is used to speed transactions in other industries.

The challenge for a company's strategic planning team is to search for technology applications in other industries and look for ways that technology can be applied to the business.

Technology—VA Hospital

The first major application of bar code scanning occurred in the retail grocery industry, as scanners enabled clerks to check out each consumer more quickly and (ideally) more accurately. The rental car industry adopted scanning technology when it looked for ways to enhance customer service by speeding the return process. When the barcode on your rental car is scanned you immediately receive a printout of the bill. No more stopping at the counter; just hop the bus to the airport.

Sue Kinnick, a long time VA Hospital nurse, noticed the auto rental company employees using the scanning equipment to produce a bill instantly. Sue wondered if the same scanning technology could be used in the VA Hospital to match doctor's orders, patients, and drugs to prevent medication errors. When the wrong medication is given to a patient, he or she often requires extensive care to rectify the situation. Medication error can result in death. Once the VA hospital installed the scanning system, medication errors plummeted by 70%. (WSJ, 12/10/2001)

Technology in taxis? Taxi Stockholm

Taxi Stockholm struggled to differentiate itself in the extremely competitive Stockholm taxi market. After evaluating several possible solutions, Taxi Stockholm decided to take advantage of the emerging GPS technology to track the location of its cabs at any time. When customers call Taxi Stockholm, its system matches the telephone number of the caller to their address. As soon as the address is verified, the GPS system locates and dispatches the nearest available cab to that address. The system then updates the caller on the estimated arrival time.

Customers flocked to the service because they could count on Taxi Stockholm to arrive promptly at the estimated time. The technology gave them confidence that the estimate would be correct. The company increased the company market share to 60% when they introduced this benefit. Copycats have not been able to regain their previous market positions. By being the early innovator in the taxi market, Taxi Stockholm gained a competitive advantage.

Progressive Insurance

Progressive, the country's third largest auto insurer, used two technology developments to set them apart from the competition.

1. First Progressive began offering consumers 'comparison rates.' Available over the phone and on its Web site, Progressive offers their quote and,

right alongside, competitors' rates for comparable coverage. The service is designed to help consumers understand that prices vary and to help them find the lowest cost alternative for them—even if it's not with Progressive. The innovative use of their Web site drove customers to try calling or going online to see where they could get the best price, giving Progressive "mindshare".

2. Progressive claims representatives use wireless communications to handle the claims process. Claims reps prepare the repair estimate—either at the customers' home, office, or even at the accident site, and transmit it to the company's mainframe. When the information is verified, the claim rep is able to print out a check to settle the claim right there on site. No waiting. This way, the customer can get their vehicle in the repair shop faster and get back on the road faster.

Progressive's savvy use of technology sets them apart in the crowded world of auto insurance. They used available technology to solve the key consumer complaints:

1. The difficulty of comparing rates from different insurance companies.
2. The time it takes to get paid for a claim.

Now Your Company – The Next Great Innovator

When your team looks for innovation, seek new ways to use your competencies, ways to solve unmet or emerging needs and preferences, and ways to use technologies proven in other industries to gain advantage in your industry. A sharp lookout for shifts in productivity, customer service, and product/service enhancements can be a key factor in developing a "first mover" advantage for your company.

As you think about innovation for your company, look around and analyze how other industries are using technology and ask yourself the questions:
1. How would this technology enhance my service or product?
2. How would this technology enhance our processes?
3. How would this technology enhance the overall customer experience?

The Easy Way to Innovate is - - the Hard Way
by Robert W. Bradford

People, quite naturally, prefer to do easy things. Easy things are – well, easy. It often seems, when we look at our businesses, that the more things we can make easy, the more profitable the company will be. To a point, this is true. If you are putting more effort than you need to into creating your product or service, the time and effort involved may well be coming right out of your bottom line. Recognizing this, most managers will put plenty of effort into taking effort out of your processes.

But wait – there's a catch. Management is not just about minimizing cost – it's also about maximizing value. Some of the effort involved in your business creates tremendous value for your customers, and chances are *you aren't even sure where the greatest value lies*.

When companies set out to innovate strategically, they often rush off in the same direction as everyone else. In many industries – especially high-tech industries – this causes markets to mature very quickly as unique specialty items that took tremendous R&D investment become "me-too" commodities. If the innovation is a compelling one that creates real, preferred value for the customer, this commoditization is almost inevitable. The only place this is unlikely to occur is when your competitors – for whatever reason – do *not* copy your valuable idea.

The concept that competitors might not copy something

that is strategically valuable seems absurd on its face. After all, why wouldn't you copy a product that enables a competitor to gain valuable market share, often at higher margins? It turns out there are several very good reasons why a competitor might not do this. First – and this is one of the best – competitors sometimes are simply unable to copy a new product or service. The reason this is a very good situation should be clear – if you do something valuable for your customers that your competition cannot copy, you have created something that looks an awful lot like a strategic competency, which we all know is practically a license to print money. Unfortunately, this situation is less common than we would like to think. Additionally, we may embark upon a project expecting that our competitors will be unable to copy us only to find out, much to our disappointment, that this is not true. The worst thing about such a disappointment is that it is likely to turn up only after we have spent strategically significant amounts of time and money. However, if you want to avoid this disappointment, there is a key choice you must tend towards in your strategic decision-making: you need to focus your efforts on the hard stuff. The reason that difficulty becomes strategically attractive here is that it increases the likelihood that our competitors, in fact, cannot copy our innovations.

The second reason why competitors may not copy us is that

they choose not to. Why would this happen? Basically, competitors are likely to decide against copying good ideas when they think that either (1) the cost is too high, (2) the payoff is too small or (3) they just don't like the idea. Let's examine how a competitor might reach these conclusions.

First, the cost being too high: naturally, the cost might actually be too high, but this is one we don't want to use, because it would hurt us, too. Much preferred would be that the competitor's perceived cost is too high, while our actual cost is not. There are two key ways to hit this mark: one, choose innovation projects that appear to be expensive at first – and turn out not to be, or two, choose projects where you have some actual cost advantage in the innovation process. Both of these options require that you know a great deal about your product, service or processes – companies that are just dabbling will not likely succeed in either.

The second reason a competitor might decide not to copy your strategic innovation is that they perceive the payoff as being to low.

The final reason a competitor may decide against copying you is one of my favorites. Sometimes, a competitor just doesn't like the direction you are going. The beauty of this is that you competitors effectively leave you with a monopoly by making this choice.

The third reason why competitors may not copy us is that they are prevented from copying by someone else. Usually, this is a legal situation (as in the case of a technology covered by patents), but it may be driven by other forces as well. While many companies rely on this tactic in support of their strategic dominance, it has one major flaw: the prevention that makes this tactic effective is outside of your control, and may only be temporary in nature. The very best use for this tactic is to give you a head start on the next innovation, since – at some point – it may be possible to get so far ahead of your competition that they effectively give up on the direction you have taken.

Integrating innovation with your strategy process
by M. Dana Baldwin

Fostering innovation in a company is a delicate balancing act. On one hand innovation needs free-wheeling creativity to spawn ideas, but it also needs a structure and discipline to bring the creative concepts to fruition. Too much creativity and you get lots of ideas but no results. Too much structure and you may never get an idea worth pursuing.

Innovation is rarely linear. By its nature, it is full of unexpected developments and surprises. It is very difficult to mandate that we develop a break-through idea within 12 months. But while any given project may be hard to predict, highly innovative companies like FedEx, Walgreen Drug or Avery Dennison are able develop a consistent string of new concepts that drive their business and the market forward at a predictable pace.

Innovation is a general term applied to many types of creative activities. When a company is trying to be more innovative they could be talking about anything from improving customer service to hatching new product ideas. To clarify things a bit further we subscribe the working definition developed by James Bryan Quinn; "Innovation is the first reduction to practice of an idea in a culture"

Innovation and strategy both seek to move a company forward and make it more successful. It is important that these two processes are compatible and work together to a common vision for a company. Here are a few tips that will help you integrate innovation with your strategy process.

First: You need to pick a type of innovation process that is correct for your company. The result of this process could include a new product, a new service, a break-through in R & D or the reinvention of a current strategy concept, yours or a competitor's. You need to look at the tools your company has to use in this process. What strengths can this process take advantage of? What weaknesses should you stay away from?

Second: Once you have decided your general goals, you should look at your organization to see where and how this process should be initiated. Does your organizational structure support the innovation process you have selected? What are the organization's strengths and weaknesses? Will the culture within the company support the innovation development procedures? What is the tolerance for risk within the company? Will the management team allow highly speculative research, or is it more conservative in its approach? The important point here is that the level of risk tolerance must be compatible with the overall philosophy of the company, or the dissonance could doom the project.

Third: What is the time scale for such a development process? This will depend on a number of factors. First among these is the size and complexity of the project. If the development project is an extension or minor modification of an existing product or service, the time scale could well be a few months up to a year in length. Conversely, a major R & D project could take years to complete, with a huge commitment of personnel and other resources. Your team should determine the size and complexity of the development and pick a time-line which is appropriate and compatible with the scope of the project.

Fourth: Decide on what measures should be appropriate to spur creativity in your team.

Having established the relationship between strategy and innovation, you can then work on stimulating the team to think of innovations that could drive your strategy. Examples include (but are not limited to):

Smart Bombing: This involves analyzing your company as if you were going to create it from scratch. What have you done well? What have you done that could have been done much better? What have you been doing which you never should have started, or, assuming the competitive environment changed, should not now be doing. What are your Strategic Competencies – those few combinations of skills, processes and knowledge that give you one or more sustainable competitive advantages, because they add value for your customers, provide differentiation from your

PRESEI

PRODUCTS

or

SERVICES

P
R
E
S
E
N
T

N
E
W

CURRENT BUSINESS

- Add New Customers
- Increase sales to current custc

AUGMENT

- Internal product development
- License from others
- Sell products of others
- Merge or acquire
- Joint venture

OPPORTUNITIES

MARKETS

NEW

AUGMENT

- Internal market development
- License to others
- Sell through others
- Merge or acquire
- Joint Venture

DIVERSIFY

- Various combinations of augmentation activities

competition and are difficult to copy. Step outside of your company and pretend you are your most formidable competitor. How would you then attack your own company to take advantage of weaknesses and to overcome strengths?

Map your competition: Where are your competitors strong and where are there holes of which you could take advantage with some development and a determined effort to exploit the openings.

Extend your Strategic Competencies: Once you have determined your Strategic Competencies (those using the Simplified Strategic Planning process will find this on worksheet 3.2), step back to see what new things you could do which would build on these competencies. One example is Federal Express going into managing warehousing and shipping for other companies. Another is Fed Ex going into overnight computer repair servicing. Both of these activities build on their strengths in overnight shipping, information services associated with shipping and integration with similarly oriented services.

Logical Analysis: Using the General Business Strategy matrix, look at each of the four categories and analyze each to see what opportunities may present themselves as you study each one.

What can you build on that will address needs and opportunities in one or more of the four categories? How can you take advantage of the strengths you use now to reach your current customers/markets? What can you do to extend your products/services to more customers who look essentially like your existing customers? How can you sell your existing products/services to new customers who are not currently your targets? What new product or service could you sell to your existing customers? Finally, what new product or service could you develop to sell to customers you don't yet know? This is not an easy process, and can involve considerable time, effort and cost to do well. Looking at industry trends, competitors, where you think the industry will be in three, five or ten years, and at your strategic competencies should give you hints as to where you should look for new opportunities.

Ask your customers: Where better to learn what you might do that your customers might buy than to ask them? Be careful that you don't get the problem of the day. Your questions need to be sufficiently penetrating that you get to the real problems your customers are facing, and thus to the real needs they have. Most of the time, the first things you hear are not the real problems they have. You need to gently probe for their real pain, and what the possible solutions might be, in order to make this effective.

Brainstorming: While this is an obvious tactic, to be done well, this exercise needs to be structured and controlled. Someone who is not directly concerned with the content of the session should be responsible for facilitating and controlling your brainstorming discussion. Without guidance and control, the session could easily drift away from the goals of the team, with the results not justifying the time, expense or effort. The trick is to allow sufficient latitude so the team does not feel too constrained, yet to have enough control so that the discussion is focused on the general areas of interest.

One caution should be that, on occasion, a wild idea will surface which can be the real homerun you are looking for or totally impractical and worthless. Give your team sufficient freedom to put those off-the-wall ideas down, for two reasons. First, even the worst, wildest idea, while not at all practical by itself, may well be a catalyst for a great idea which could be the winner you are looking for. Second, by allowing any and all ideas to be submitted, everyone is encouraged to contribute, and your session will be more effective, more productive and, frankly, more fun. The process should screen out those concepts which don't fit your needs or capabilities, leaving those which have better possibilities for your company.

Next you need a good process to capture ideas so they may

be evaluated and filtered. (For those using Simplified Strategic Planning the worksheet on page 4.4 is an excellent tool for capturing and assessing ideas from brainstorming). You want to quickly evaluate at a base level each opportunity to see if it meets the first level needs of the company. The process is very straightforward to use. First, the team goes into a brainstorming session as discussed above. An open atmosphere is requisite for the best generation of ideas, and immediate judgment tends to intimidate those who might contribute in the absence of such judgment.

Once the team has generated all the ideas they can come up with, take a break for a few minutes to allow everyone's minds to clear. On reconvening, ask if anyone else has had any new thoughts. If anyone does have new ideas, write them down with the others on the flip charts, then proceed to the evaluation phase.

There are four criteria which must be considered.

First: Consider the potential profit impact on the company. Here one uses two assumptions: One: That the company puts full efforts into making the idea work, and Two: That the result of the idea is successful. On a scale from 10 to 1, with 10 representing a grand slam home run and a 1 representing a tiny positive increment to the bottom line, rate each opportunity as to its potential impact on the bottom line, net of costs and investment.

Second: The team immediately will try to validate the assumption just made about the first factor. One needs to judge the probability that the company can actually attain the profit impact you just selected. Using a probability percentage – we suggest you use increments no smaller than 10% — determine your best estimate as to how likely you will be successful to the degree you just selected in the first factor.

Third: Management time is one of the scarcest resources any company has. To best utilize the assets of the company, you need to estimate the impact of the opportunity on the available time of management. This is rated on a scale of High, Moderate or Low.

Fourth: One important consideration is that of what happens if the opportunity is not successfully implemented, or if it fails after being attempted. There are three types of impact which may be considered, depending on the situation. First, and most likely the most important, is the financial risk. Second is the impact on your market reputation if you try something and it fails. Third is the effect that failure could have on the morale of your personnel.

Once these four criteria have been considered and rated as

above, the team will sort each of the opportunities into one of three categories. First is a "plus", which represents those opportunities which will remain as candidates for further consideration and possible exploration and implementation, given the right sets of circumstances. Second is a "minus" which indicates that at the current time, the opportunity does not merit further consideration. Opportunities in this category do remain on our list, however, for further consideration should circumstances merit at some future time. The third category is a "question mark." For any opportunity put in this category, your team has determined that more information is needed in order to put it into a "plus" or "minus" category.

To further explore this question mark category, your team should perform a detailed screening to evaluate the potential for failure of these "uncertain" opportunities (for users of Simplified Strategic Planning, worksheet 4.5, Opportunity Screening Work Sheet, serves to raise a series of questions for the purpose of allowing the team to minimize the exposure to failure). When over 80% of all new product introductions fail in the marketplace, it makes good sense to run any questionable ideas through a screening process which is aimed at minimizing your exposure to failure. While it is not a guarantee of success, it usually will help eliminate failures before they become expensive. In addition, any "plus" opportunity may also be evaluated using a similar screening worksheet.

Finally, if someone on the team feels very strongly that one of the opportunities which the team rated as a "minus" has potential, he or she may undertake the worksheet, playing the role of champion. If, in the process of filling out the sheet, the author determines at any time that the opportunity is <u>not</u> appropriate at this time, the exercise may be terminated at will. Otherwise, when one is filling out the sheet, the exercise should be completed, and a recommendation made to the team.

Once the team has selected the opportunities which are viable candidates for the team's consideration – the plusses and those question marks which resulted in being voted plusses – the team needs to place each item in priority order, so the company can address them in the best sequence based on the availability of personnel and financing.

When the team has sequenced the opportunities and decided which ones to start on first, the next task is to put in place a formal process to exploit each one. A written action plan is an ideal vehicle for development of innovative ideas. (For users of Simplified Strategic Planning, the action plan is shown on worksheet 7.x) The action plan consists of the individual steps, in sequence, which must be performed in order to accomplish the objective.

To get started, write a simple outline or flow chart of the approximate process that will be followed to accomplish the task. This helps in two ways. First, it allows the authors to visualize the general procedure that will be followed. Second, it allows the authors to understand the other parts of the company that may be affected by this procedure, and to potentially involve people from those areas in the writing of the actual plan. Pull the appropriate people together and write out each action step. Put them in order and assign resources: people, time and money. Finish the final draft and allow it to sit for up to a week. Review and revise the plan if appropriate, then submit to the overall team for their input and revisions.

In this process, it is incumbent on the action plan team (and later for the whole team) to make every effort to improve and extend the effectiveness of each idea for innovation. The goal should be to develop the most practical application of each concept, and to implement it in the most effective way, identifying any road blocks and dealing with them in the process. Creativity in dealing with road blocks is needed, as the roadblocks can derail the innovation process unless each is dealt with effectively.

How does one deal with a road block that springs up in the

middle of an innovation development process? There is no single answer, as each situation is likely unique to the situation. In general, creativity is encouraged through brainstorming and/or logical analysis to determine possible solutions. One key here is to not get locked into a single approach.

Once the team has ideas on how to approach the problem, rank the solutions and select the best approach. Develop the solution or solutions to the problem and select the best solution. During the development process, don't forget to keep the marketplace in mind. Whenever feasible, try to validate your potential solutions with selected, trusted customers. Use them as your unpaid consultants to help evaluate the effectiveness and appropriateness of your proposed solutions. Bounce your concepts off them, listen to their responses, determine what improvements they suggest are appropriate for incorporation into the prototype. Once the final configuration has been determined, write out an action plan for trials and for final roll-out. Use the same approach as outlined above to establish the roll out plan, including prototyping, selected customer trials and final evaluation. Finally, evaluate the effectiveness of the process your team has followed to get to this point, and incorporate the lessons learned when you do this again the next time.

While an innovation process can certainly stand on its own, it is more powerful if it is integrated into the strategic planning process and on going management of a company.

Innovative measures

by Thomas E. Ambler

Are your profits getting pounded because of pricing pressures? If so, you have lots of company and it's good company. In most markets commoditization of products and services is running rampant as a result of the confluence of a number of major forces, including global markets and supply, ease of gaining information about purchase alternatives and pervasiveness of a Wal-mart purchasing mentality. Specialty buying behavior with its premium prices has not disappeared. It has become generally less lucrative. Today, even Specialty Buyers, who have traditionally placed highest weight on high quality and superior features and benefits in their value equation, have shifted additional weight to price levels that are at least in the same universe as the lowest price. So what can you do? Is it hopeless? Of course not! One alternative used by even niche players is to devote increasingly more attention to commodity strategies focused on removing cost from their core products and services. Although this may be easy at first, it becomes progressively harder and that takes real innovation. Another major strategic alternative focuses on making old products new through customer-driven functional improvements, but that takes real innovation. Yet another strategy, compelled by either commoditization or desire for growth, calls for developing entirely new products and services to replace or complement old ones, but that too takes real innovation. Finally, you can develop a totally new business concept that turns your existing market on its ear (AKA disruptive) or permits you to enter a whole new market. But again, that too takes real innovation. So, no matter how you cut it, continued SUCCESS in virtually any business TAKES REAL INNOVATION. Innovation must pervade every aspect of your business—your business model, product development, operations, sales and support.

Making Innovation Happen

Innovation can "just happen" serendipitously, but don't count on it. The kind of innovation you need for continued success requires intentionally providing the right inputs and transforming them into valuable innovative outcomes. You need an "Innovation Machine" comprised of the right processes, organization and culture. The diagram below illustrates such an "Innovation Machine" with its typical inputs and outputs. It represents this author's boiled-down, visualization of much of the collective wisdom from a number of innovation experts. Please take a moment to absorb and understand the nature of this "Innovation Machine."

The use of the word "Machine" could imply that innovation is a science with inherent predictability. Nothing could be further from reality. This "Machine" at best suggests that a set of probabilistic input/output relationships exists. These relationships, even though often just vaguely defined

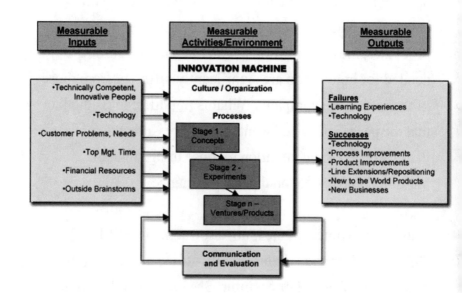

Measurable Inputs	Measurable Activities/Environment	Measurable Outputs

INNOVATION MACHINE

Culture / Organization

Processes

Stage 1 - Concepts

Stage 2 - Experiments

Stage n – Ventures/Products

Measurable Inputs

•Technically Competent, Innovative People

•Technology

•Customer Problems, Needs

•Top Mgt. Time

•Financial Resources

•Outside Brainstorms

Measurable Outputs

Failures
•Learning Experiences
•Technology

Successes
•Technology
•Process Improvements
•Product Improvements
•Line Extensions/Repositioning
•New to the World Products
•New Businesses

Communication and Evaluation

hypotheses, can be used to increase the likelihood of successful innovation. Over time these hypothetical relationships should be tested and refined.

In many ways the recipes for success in innovation are very different from the ones that work for the ongoing operations of a core business. That is why successful innovation eludes so many companies. The people, the processes, the organizational structure and the culture needed for innovation are significantly different from those of the rest of the company. What is <u>not</u> different is the fact that the people involved want to be successful and, therefore, pay great attention to those things that are measured and reflect on their performance.

Consistent winners in the innovation arena like 3M, DuPont, Pfizer and HP universally utilize metrics for their innovation efforts. For example, 3M has utilized for many years a high-level corporate metric, "Percentage of Total Revenue from products introduced in the last 5 years." They had historically set a goal of 25% and were consistently hitting it. They then jacked the goal up to 30% and shortened the period of time to 4 years to accelerate their market growth. Because this metric was so much a part of the culture of 3M's innovation teams, it took only 2 years to exceed the new goal.

HP utilizes **BET** (break-even time for each new product development project). It is desirable because it focuses the attention of the innovation team on 3 critical elements— (1) the Investment in the development; (2) the Profitability equation for the product; and (3) the Total Time until the accumulated profits pay back the investment.

Although many excellent examples could be cited, it should be no great revelation that properly used metrics can be great motivators in the world of innovation just as they are elsewhere.

One excellent, high-level overall measure of innovation is the **Wealth Creation Index** (recommended by Gary Hamel in his book, *Leading the Revolution*). It measures a company's relative capacity to invent new business concepts and create new wealth against that of its competitive "Domain." (Domain is defined as a relevant, broad set of existing and potential competitors, including upstream and downstream value chain players and those who possess similar core competencies.) Innovation <u>is</u> intended to increase the Market Value of a company. The winning company creates Market Value faster than its competitors.

WCI = Your % <u>Current</u> Share of the Total Market Value of all Companies in your Domain + Your % <u>Previous</u> Share of the Total Market Value of all Companies in your Domain

Your **WCI** should be greater than 1.0 for you to be better than the average competitor.

Conceptually, this metric has a lot of merit because it incorporates both the Market Value contribution of radical innovation and the change (quite possibly a decline) in the market value of the core business in the absence of radical innovation. It covers the fact that some firms have a greater need for innovation to sustain their Market Value and must, therefore, be more successful with their investment in innovation than their competitors. Unfortunately, **WCI** defies practicality for all but those large firms whose domain is largely publicly held with market values determined by the stock market.

A more practical, but less elegant overall company measure of the success of innovation is

Return on Innovation = (Cumulative 3-year net profits from commercialized new products) + (Cumulative 3-year new product total expenditures for commercialized, failed or killed products)

Note that, although this particular metric relates to new products, a similar metric can be utilized for cost reduction innovation.

Ideally, the Measures of Success or Metrics appropriate for

your innovation would relate to <u>outcomes</u> in the marketplace. Consider the following company-wide, outcome-related metrics (recommended by Thomas Kuczmarski in his book, *Innovation, Leadership Strategies For The Competitive Edge*):

- **Survival Rate** = # of commercialized new products still in the market + total # of new products commercialized

- **Success Rate** = # of new products exceeding their original 3-year revenue forecast + Total # of new products commercialized

- **R&D Innovation Effectiveness Ratio** = Cumulative 3-year Gross Profits from commercialized new products + Cumulative 3-year R&D expenditure solely for new products

- **Innovation Sales Ratio** = Total 3rd year revenues from commercialized new products + Total annual revenues

- **Innovation Portfolio Mix** = Percentage of new products (# and revenue) commercialized by type, where type includes incremental product improvements, product line extensions, new-to-the-world products, new business concepts, etc.

- **Innovation Revenues Per Employee** = total
  cumulative 3-year annual revenues from
  commercialized new products + total equivalent full-
  time employees devoted to innovation initiatives

- % Of Sales From Proprietary Products

Unfortunately, development cycle times may be too long
and the number of stages of development too numerous for
you to rely solely on <u>outcomes</u> for measuring and
motivating innovation. As a result, you will likely need to
add metrics for both the activities within the "Innovation
Machine" and the levels of its key inputs. Such measures
may also be crucial to gaining a clearer understanding of
how your "Innovation Machine" transforms various inputs
into innovation outcomes.

You cannot afford to measure everything. So what should
you measure? Certainly you don't want to track a metric
whose cost outweighs its benefits. But you can't always
know ahead of time what the benefits are. One fruitful
approach to identify what is worth measuring is to address
the question, "What does it take to be a Winner at
innovation?" In other words, "what are the key ingredients
and what are their relative importance?" In the popular book

Simplified Strategic Planning, authors Robert Bradford and Peter Duncan describe one our company's process exercises known as Winner's Profile. This exercise can be applied to the 2 questions just posed. It will identify the few, most important innovation ingredients—the obvious candidates for appropriate metrics.

In addition to key metrics for individual inputs to the "Innovation Machine," you may want to consider including:

- **Innovation Portfolio Investment Mix** = Cumulative 3-yr. expenditures for each of the major types of innovation such as incremental product improvements, product line extensions, new-to-the-world products, new business concepts, etc. + Cumulative 3-yr. total innovation expenditures

- (This fits well with the **Innovation Portfolio Mix** defined above.)

Useful Transformation Process/Organization/Culture Activity metrics include:

- **Time to Market** with the next generation of products

- **Process Pipeline Flow** = # of new product concepts in each stage of the development process at year-end

- **Yield at Each Stage** = the % of projects that graduate from the concept stage to the feasibility stage

- **Cost At Each Stage** = Average cost /project at each stage or % of total development cost at each stage

- **Average Cycle Time to Complete a Stage**

- **Existence of Crucial Cultural/Organizational Characteristics** (these might simply be 0-1 measures for things like management acceptance of failures, CEO involvement in innovation, compensation that fosters entrepreneurship or real progress in developing Innovation as a core competency)

Some of these metrics can be benchmarked against other companies that are innovation leaders or competitors. Consider setting targets that reflect benchmarks or support the strategic needs of your company. Metrics related to input levels and outcomes are good candidates for targets. Some metrics will not lend themselves to targets and outside comparisons but still have value. Others will have meaning only in terms of their trend over time or when analyzed in combination with other metrics.

Systems that link specific people and teams to specific

metrics need to put in place. Ideally, these systems promote entrepreneurial behavior with its willingness to risk failure so often associated with innovation success. The achievement of metrics, accompanied by celebration and rewards, can prove to be a highly motivational, short-term surrogate for the real goal of actually reaching fruition on new developments—often a long and always tenuous journey.

The "Innovation Machine" is different for every company. Its strategic purpose is different, the level of importance of each input is different, the processes, organization and culture are different and the number and length of stages in the development process are different. For example, there is a world of difference between a pharmaceutical company that averages 12 years to develop a new drug and a software firm where development may be measured in weeks. Likewise, there are major differences in the innovation processes that fit a giant's R&D lab environment and those of a shop floor R&D environment of a smaller company or the unique environment of your company. As result, we can never claim that "one size system of metrics fits all." We can, however, claim that the broad types of metrics and key factors of innovation that should be considered for measurement are much the same for all companies. Therefore, view the metrics offered above as an inviting "smorgasbord" of possibilities.

So, if innovation is a strategic necessity for your survival or competitive advantage, you need every tool you can lay your hands on. "Innovative Measures" are among the best. Pick some good ones and get started!

/